LIVING AT TH

The Morse Poetry Prize
Edited by Guy Rotella

ALLISON FUNK

Living at the Epicenter

THE 1995 MORSE
POETRY PRIZE
SELECTED AND
INTRODUCED BY
SONIA SANCHEZ

Northeastern University Press
BOSTON

Northeastern University Press

Library of Congress Cataloging-in-Publication Data

Funk, Allison.
   Living at the epicenter / Allison Funk.
      p.   cm.—(Morse Poetry Prize)
   ISBN 1-55553-247-0 (paper : alk. paper)
   I. Title. II. Series.
PS3556.U62L58   1995
811'.54—dc20   95-32437

Designed by Ann Twombly

Composed in Weiss by Graphic Composition, Athens, Georgia. Printed and bound by Thomson-Shore, Inc., Dexter, Michigan. The paper is Glatfelter Supple Opaque Recycled, an acid-free stock.

MANUFACTURED IN THE UNITED STATES OF AMERICA
99   98   97   96   95   5   4   3   2   1

for my sons, Josh and Adam,
and for George

ACKNOWLEDGMENTS

Grateful acknowledgment is made to the following magazines in which the poems in this book were originally published, sometimes in slightly different versions.

Drumvoices Revue	"Assateague Island"
	"Midnight"
Graham House Review	"Cicada"
The Journal	"Wandering Prayer"
	"When the Light Changes"
Mississippi Valley Review	"Living at the Epicenter"
	"The Wreck of the Essex, 1819"
	"Redbud"
	"Flowstone"
	"Women"
Poetry	"Turning Forty"
	"After Dark"
	"Faultline"
	"Blondin"
	"Sea Change"
Poetry Northwest	"Bioluminescence"
	"Backstroke"
	"August: A Lunar Eclipse"
	"The Moons of Uranus"
	"Snake Road"
	"Insomnia"

"Stalactites" first appeared in the *Cimarron Review* and is reprinted here with the permission of the Board of Regents for Oklahoma State University, holders of the copyright.

"Lessons in Mimicry" appeared in a limited edition printing published by the Molheid Press in 1991.

"After Dark" was included in *The Best American Poetry, 1994*.

The comment in the epigraph of "Another World" appeared in the *New York Times*, March 29, 1994, p. A20, in an article by Peter Applebome titled "Across the Tornado Belt, The Rubble Is Real, But the Losses Are So Hard to Grasp."

The epigraph in "Wandering Prayer" is an excerpt from pp. 22 and 23 of David Pownall's novel *The White Cutter* (New York: Viking Penguin, 1988).

My deep thanks to the National Endowment for the Arts, whose generous support provided me with a year to write. I am also grateful to Southern Illinois University at Edwardsville for two summer fellowships that enabled me to finish this book. I want to thank Howard Levy, Eric Pankey, Jennifer Atkinson, Jason Sommer, Steve Schreiner, Jeff Hamilton, and my husband, George Soule, for their advice and support.

Contents

I V

Introduction

What does it mean, to live at the epicenter? How does the body compensate as one finds oneself at the focal point, in the heart of the storm? What new parts of oneself might one meet, once confronted with the disembodiment of surroundings or circumstances? Poet Allison Funk wants us to wonder how relevant it is to hear the answer of Eliza Bryan of New Madrid, Missouri. She wrote about a series of earthquakes that hit the region in late 1811 and early 1812:

> 2 A.M. she wakes to a babel of trees,
>   wind and wildfowl, stones
> and a hollow thunder confounded.
>   Hoarse. Vibrations.
>   Family and neighbors
>
> reeling in the darkness of sinking acres.
>   Shock after shock
> until morning—
>   an uncontrollable passion
>   seizes everything:
>
> the Mississippi
>   like an animal in heat,
> oaks thrusting at one another,
>   the houses come unfastened.
>   Heaved from their nests,
>
> birds land
>   on her shoulders and head.
> Wings in her face.
>   Odor of sulfur.
>   Shower of dust.

It is relevant, as seen in California today, in the Mississippi's recent acts of rage. By bearing witness to such incidents we sample our own ability to manage natural and unnatural disasters: those points where we must navigate, amid cruel reversals, the possibilities that emerge as a "furious river/murders its banks." The Mississippi runs through the book as well as the title poem, a persistently powerful force that makes its voice from all lives affected by its living. The river is a symbol of the unanticipated, for we hear her pen say:

> how in the middle of one night
> the world we've known
> can open up without warning,
> all of nature
> begin speaking in tongues.

Inside the poet's laboratory she pursues the idea of reversals, dualities, illusions. She is curious about the wonderment of life's seeming order, once it has been disturbed. Her tone is often that of a confidante, dispensing secrets, but also one who wants an active listener, a participant, as she discovers the jewel that sometimes comes out of upheaval,

> like the truth that, out,
> casts everything we thought we ever knew
> in doubt.

Images from the natural world are rarely far from these poems; the volume is made richer because of it. Its journey of questions is skillfully meshed with gritty footsteps, luminous wings, and bodies of water. At times the poet becomes chronicler of what the water sees, knows, touches, and changes.

> With it came the secrets
> of where it had been.
> So the men

who discovered the green river
ten miles wide in the blue
current of the Gulf Stream

could almost see the Midwest
as if it had been their land. . . .

There is a distinct desire in the work for reunification of earthly forces and human forces. Several poems affirm a level of dialogue, relationship, and connectedness between the two. Through earthquake, flood, or even the slow kiss of erosion, power and meaning are traded back and forth between men and women on one hand, rock and water on the other.

Finally, what works best in these pieces is the binding together of conscious and unconscious through carefully constructed images. As a woman jumps from a window to live, the image is woven with the thought: what is it to be "an eighth, sixteenth note / quickening as she falls"? As we pivot between the poet's absorbing eye and the interpretations of her vision that loom in the mind, there is room to consider the idea of the epicenter again; the idea of a necessary volatility; a means of measuring one's resiliency against the world.

SONIA SANCHEZ

I

≈ Stalactites —

a cylindrical or conical deposit usually of calcite or aragonite, projecting downward from the roof of a caverns as a result of the dripping of mineral-rich water

A child could snap one easily in her hand,
but the day an earthquake
shook the boulders from the hills,

not one was broken.
The people in the caverns below
heard nothing but distant thunder,

while above, struck dumb,
as if it were his own heart convulsing,
farmer after farmer ran from his field.

It was not the end of the world,
but it might have been
for all they knew below

where crystal formations, milky, gold,
and manganese blue, hung
like ornaments for their pleasure.

The pure white eyeless fish
swam around their boat
in astonishing numbers,

as unconscious of danger as bees
circumnavigating a garden of flowers.
And so they drifted on,

as if blessed, beyond harm
between the glittering walls
lit by their candles.

Imagination can take us only so far.
But I know the rest of the way:
how, at first, the pilgrims surfacing

3

near where the underground river
spills forth as a spring
were almost blinded by a light

as wondrous as what they'd seen within.
Then, slowly, as their eyes adjusted,
through the deciduous green

they saw it all,
all the damage done,
as if dreaming again.

🌿 The Moons of Uranus

Often what is darkest, say, the moons
of Uranus, we shine names upon.
Against last night's argument or indifference
we wake, lift the shade and think
Monday or *Tuesday* or *May*.
At winter's solstice it's *Christmas*
or the lilting syllables of *Hanukkah*,
each one a candle.
Before they are born we name our children,
blinding ourselves to the perils,
blessing their passage to light.
My Adam, my Joshua.

And so the icy moons of Uranus
with their frozen valleys and cliffs,
their frigid zones that do not glow
are Ophelia, Desdemona, Rosalind.
Even from his grave the poet speaks.
And others with the storm of ashes
nearly upon them say *Jesus*.
A couple in the theater
wish disbelief away as the curtain rises,
while outside in the autumn night
the heartsick swallow the harvest moon
like a tablet.

We resemble the scientists
who have given the barren moons of Uranus
the beautiful names of lovers—
Miranda, Titania, dead Juliet.
In the dark of our house
you call me Sweetheart.
I still call you Love.

Insomnia

It took to fire like a lover.
A careless match, a windblown ember

dropped onto the drained swampland
dark with carbon,

and the muck married the fire.
Cursed with perfect memory

a mint field in northern Indiana
could burn for years.

People joked that anything could provoke it:
lightning miles away, a word, wanton or ill chosen,

a man and a woman in the loam.
But with a black disposition

and a temper that flared
behind the plow, my great-grandfather

could find no humor in this,
much less in his name, German for spark.

Tonight what's still burning
filters up through the porous layers,

surfacing as a telltale haze,
and I cannot sleep for knowing

all the green mint in the world
cannot conceal it.

We begin by accident
and smoulder as long as we last.

✍ Lessons in Mimicry

THE BEE ORCHID

How like a kind of love
this seems, the bee in wind
laden with the orchid's scent,
driven by instinct, brushing past
the flesh-white outer petals
toward dusk. The decoy so much
like the abdomen of the female,
he alights on the labellum
and begins his dance.
What a whirlwind! A dust devil
of pollen spinning everywhere, confetti
coming down, constellating at last
on the bee's sticky limbs.
Imagine the orchid
that feels nothing.

7

THE ANT MIMIC

She could be magnificent,
but fidgety, busy, always running,
her fourth pair of legs held together
in front, looking to any predator
like antennae, she's mistaken for an ant.
Even her natural fullness is constricted to a waist.
Would you guess that when she dreams
she's a diva
at the center of her web
glistening like the highest notes
of an aria over the heads
of all those who listen,
rapt, overcome by her lamentation.

THE FALSE CORAL

Now study the coral snake's rings,
its black, yellow and vermilion,
practice burrowing as the snake does,
preferring the cool privacy of the dark
to the dangers of air. Remember
the taste of venom? Poor false coral,
still innocuous, shy harlequin.
Such disguises the frightened assume:
a man lies; a woman wears a mask.
This ring, when will you take it off?
Fool's gold, you call it.

THE FIREFLY

How can you stop before you learn
the last lesson of deception?
With a twist the lie turns
from self-preservation to aggression.
When the firefly signs in light
she loves him,
the grass is wet, and danger
seems as far away as the unblinking moon.
How well you imagine her secrecy,
her hunger at the moment she inflicts the wound.
But after his light goes out, afterwards,
what does she do in the dark?

✍ Sea Change

After the flood, fresh water
green as the fields had been
in early spring

traveled a thousand five hundred miles
from the sunken farms,
and, like the snakes that invaded homes

as the floodwaters rose,
flowed into the salty Atlantic:
the Mississippi come to the Keys.

With it came the secrets
of where it had been.
So the men

who discovered the green river
ten miles wide in the blue
current of the Gulf Stream

could almost see the Midwest
as if it had been their land,
their homes erased

as the moon in eclipse
absents itself in stages:
first a crescent in shadow,

quarter moon, half; threshold,
lintel, windows and eaves darkening
until the whole house goes under.

Later, it seemed to them
as far away as the moon.
Florida to the flood, fresh water

to that other world of the sea.
But as the cells of the body
gossip to one another like neighbors

spreading this and that;
as one failure begets another;
as the pain of a woman whose breast,

also like that moon in shadow,
belongs to us all, your hunger,
his death—it keeps coming back to them

like the truth that, out,
casts everything we thought we ever knew
in doubt.

Assateague Island

She stands still so long
I wonder what keeps her in the shallow water
of the salt marsh, moving nowhere.

Everything else is leaning
toward something. Grass
and gulls in the wind off the bay,

the breakers less than a mile
from here on the ocean side.
The way one leaf in the crown of a tree

catches the sun,
she is like that, translucent
and without volition.

Meanwhile, the other
unbridled mares and stallions
blur beyond her;

dunes and shore birds,
the grace notes of waves,
everything's spinning around

this dappled horse,
as if in the midst of all the shimmering
only she is unsure of her freedom.

Feral. In the mouth it may feel
like fear. But turn from it,
try turning from it now.

✎ Backstroke

At first it is colder than I think I can bear,
but I go down anyway, go under,
and begin to move as if borne through the first passage

in a pool that tastes faintly of salt,
wondering if it's true the self is no polestar,
that we reinvent ourselves

like the grass. My pain
could be that storm of mayflies
lifting off the river for a day,

ephemera, they're named, *ephemerella*.
Even Polaris is not fixed. Years after us,
north will be marked by another star.

The water, when rent, mends itself—
this glitter, broken by thrashing swimmers,
repairs its silver net, forgets

faster than I who have chosen to swim on my back,
always looking at what I have left.
I count my laps, each invocation

and amen. My arms are like children:
how easily they tire, would sleep.
But I keep forcing them over my head,

insisting on an architecture
raised and ruined until, nearly naked,
I'm liquid in this crucible.

August: A Lunar Eclipse

Lately I have felt myself disappearing
the way the moon becomes a copper ghost
when the earth casts its shadow upon it.

This can happen when we leave someone.
Though, in truth, it must have begun before:
the steadiest, almost imperceptible

erosion that wears a boulder
down to nothing. Ice, wind, water
can do it, enough deception.

For years, without knowing it,
I was the magician's assistant.
The woman who vanishes on cue in a closet.

I may even have come to believe
I did not exist
without his tapping.

Then one night, as quickly as the moon
moves through all its phases
in a matter of hours, it was over.

That the moon returns alone
from behind the shadow, whole again,
seems a false ending, another sleight of hand.

II

🌿 Living at the Epicenter

*Eliza Bryan, of New Madrid, Missouri, wrote
one of the few surviving accounts of the series
of earthquakes that shook the region in late
1811 and early 1812.*

2 A.M. she wakes to a babel of trees,
    wind and wildfowl, stones
and a hollow thunder confounded.
    Hoarse. Vibrations.
       Family and neighbors

reeling in the darkness of sinking acres.
    Shock after shock
until morning—
    an uncontrollable passion
       seizes everything:

the Mississippi
    like an animal in heat,
oaks thrusting at one another,
    the houses come unfastened.
       Heaved from their nests,

birds land
    on her shoulders and head.
Wings in her face.
    Odor of sulfur.
       Shower of dust.

*

Later, she wondered who cared
      for her grief, what point
remembering the night
      the Mississippi flowed backwards,
         erupting like artillery.

Boats torn from their moorings,
      New Madrid's women and men
spilling in every direction.
      But the wrecked boats covering the river
         would not vanish from memory.

In one, a lady and six children,
      all lost.
Flatboat, raft, all the tenuous breaths,
      the young cottonwoods
         broken with such regularity

from a distance
      they might look like a work of art.
Not this faithlessness
      of hundreds of acres,
         a river's bad blood.

If only the intervals
      between the aftershocks
were longer,
      if she didn't see
         as if underwater—

*

Then, again
dead animals and household belongings
litter the fields,
the furious river
murders its banks,

and she is stumbling miles
waist deep in blood-warm water—
where is there dry land?
When she holds out her arms
to the children

silt runs through her fingers.
Borderless,
nothing's familiar.
Yard, road.
Others, self.

*

21

Stop moving.
    The leafless branches outside
keep shifting,
    she cannot focus,
        present capsizing into past.

Sometimes it's as muddy to her
    as the river she lives on,
but there must have been signs.
    Maybe the passenger pigeons
      arriving suddenly

like the Pharoah's locusts, swarming,
    in the fields, hundreds in a single tree.
And earlier (was it June?)
    grey squirrels in thousands
      drowned trying to cross the river.

Her memory returns like a fever,
    the hailstones
that beat the blighted crops.
    Summer? Spring?
      The seasons all unmoored.

How was it she didn't see it coming,
    she asks herself,
remembering the eclipse
    of the moon, autumn's comet
      and the monster born between its legs.

*

A great blue heron
      starts up out of the wetlands slowly,
looking broken at first,
      long legs trailing
            before, heavy winged, it flies.

Another sign, she thinks,
      dreaming the bird
in the balmy dark, the river
      she drifts in.
            Some mornings

it takes the earth's tremors
      to rouse her in her new home
on the higher ground of the bluff.
      After a year, nothing steady,
            nothing to be trusted.

What does she think will change
      if she puts it all down?
Still, bending over the page,
      she tries to tell
            what she's learned:

how in the middle of one night
      the world we've known
can open up without warning,
      all of nature
            begin speaking in tongues.

III

 *"The Golden Key"*

after *Grimm's*

What's the point of telling
the story again? Still,
I keep coming back to it

through ghostweed and autumn,
the flush of hyacinth, the bleeding heart
of all those summers after,

each time returning to the night
in the forest behind my house
where I'd gone to gather some wood.

Above, a woodpecker
reminded me of my ax,
the chopping to do when I returned,

but cold as it was
and my errand done, I decided
not to go home.

You could say any choice
is a key, but the one
I found in the snow—that trefoil

like a church window
wedded to its long grooved end—
was brighter than anything

I could will
into sight: lamp, star,
the fire I might have made

before everything vanished
in my rapture of digging
down through the top layers of snow

27

I tossed like confetti
in the air, and deeper,
shoveling with bare hands

the dirt frozen for months.
I kicked the resisting earth
in a crazed tantrum and dance

beneath the distracted crimson of that bird
before lifting the iron box
like a stone from some watery body.

No moon that night,
the fire still unlit,
so, at first, not finding the keyhole,

I hated the woodpecker
that knew just where to tap
for the insect under the layers of bark.

And worse, even when I found it
and turned the key around
once, twice, again and again,

I could not open that box.
The house still winks
at me as it did through the trees

that night before I went home,
my fingers frozen around the key.
It was not what I might have found

in that chest, some treasure
that would have blessed me
with another life. I know this.

It's what was inside my house,
what I tried to leave that night,
I keep coming back to that.

✎ The Wreck of the Essex, 1819

How could you understand
we had no choice except to draw lots?
When it fell to my cabin-boy
I started forward and cried out
My lad, my lad, if you don't like your lot,
I'll shoot the first man that touches you.
But half starved, my little Isaac
quietly lay his head on the gunnel.
When I saw his heart was smaller
than cobblestones on the streets of Nantucket,
the coral white of its houses
no match for the immaculate bones
of his hands—
my head is on fire with the recollection.

But it is another story I tell.
Of how I saw everything rising there:
the yeasty sea, all the fish
coming to the surface. Forget the fire
kindled on the ballast-sand of that little boat;
we lived like a family,
seven in the miniature craft left to us
after the whale bludgeoned our ship,
the rest of the crew lost in rough weather,
our beef and last biscuit consumed.

Taking my turn at rowing while the others slept
I could read the twisted forms of each
as well as I could my wife's
on sheets thousands of miles away.
I'm sure that we loved one another
all of the time.

Turning Forty

Lovers, all the drifting continents, are one
in the imagined world, Pangaea.
There, the hip of Africa
beats against the coast of Brazil.
Birds rain over the shared plains
of Eurasia and North America.
Mother, father. How long ago it seems.
Two hundred million years at least
since I left that fertile valley.
And still, the sea floor is spreading,
setting my loved countries adrift.
Mapmaker, palm reader, I turn to you
and the ancients, who, seeing between
islands of stars, linked,
like silversmiths,
Andromeda, her Perseus.

✒ *Flowstone*

You need to have been underground a long time
like the blindfish or cave cricket.
You need to have heard nothing

but water's slow dripping
through invisible openings in rock,
and the drops need to have fallen onto you

at the rate it takes a crystal to grow
in the dark. For a time
you may confuse beauty

with love. Seeing in everything
the body, or what you have known
above. So, in the cavern you've descended to

this length of vertical rock
becomes bone. Another, the curtains
you chose for a house left behind;

a cluster of grapes
filling a bowl remembered but lost.
Column, coral, and muscle.

Slowly, you will learn to call it
by no other name than its own.
Flowstone,

because stone seen without longing
or grief reflects not your brief passage
but the glowing miracles

of water and mineral
far from what coils
and lengthens under the sun.

✿ Bioluminescence

You see one flash, another
at twilight, and soon the hedges and grass
are frantic with signals: Morse
distinctive as a kiss.

One firefly near the ground clicks
four quick pulses of light;
another is an arc, then electric.
The length of the message matters:

crescendo or millisecond spike.
Hold the shutter open
and they're fireworks,
falling stars or sperm.

Bioluminescence is lush on your tongue
this balmy night in July, no moon
making the mating better.
You could lose your senses

as the lamps on a speeding ferris wheel
blur; you're riding a circle of light,
the crickets and katydids singing now,
candles in the wet pastures, at the forest's edge.

Light-headed, light-hearted, you think
of an airport at night, the lit strip blinking,
someone in the tower bidding you land
safely, safely in your borrowed wings.

But there are false lights here, also.
Mimicry, trickery.
Imagine how many fireflies are lying,
pretending consent, surprising their prey.

It's sordid plots, Harlequin romance.
Or cold light in thin air at best,
and brief. The blaze lasts just minutes,
then radiance fails altogether,

sky and living fire.
So fly beyond the wet grass,
try to wish hunger away.
Do your imitation of a stone

or the tree on the lawn
that has just gone black.

✒ *Wandering Prayer*

The female Cistercian architect . . . had tried to
construct a roomy, airy space behind the altar
that could be used for what the women at Kirlees
called "wandering prayer."
       —David Pownall, The White Cutter

Because the world was terrible
and the wild pigs in the forest
real, they sketched painstaking lines
of foliage on stone pillars

and made of their church
a forest indoors. How lissome
marble became, how like the young ash trees
beyond the convent wall.

The English sisters strolled
among the stone saplings,
then devised figures and steps,
ringing their handmade trees.

Wandering prayer, they called their dance
to banish the devils,
as Jesus had the swine.
Meanwhile, beyond the wall, larkspur

and fern flourished among the rocks.
Evergreen, dust and dung.
And sometimes through the convent panes
snow fell far away.

Still, better the colorless stone foliage
without seasons, the sisters agreed.
The pigs would run right through you
if you opened the door.

Sometimes when the abbess wasn't looking,
as frivolity was not allowed,
the sisters would chase one another
behind the altar,

flapping their arms like black birds
in their habits. Faster and faster,
making themselves the wind,
then birds again, *caw, caw,*

caught! they screamed
when they'd pinned one against a tree.
How little they remembered
of sacrifice and modesty then,

the captured sister
squealing with delight,
the others squawking,
dizzily turning circles around her

as if this were the end of all their prayer
and art. *Gone to heaven,*
the stuck one cried out,
and the game would begin again.

 *Redbud*

1.

Who misnamed this tree?

Deeper than lavender,
though the lilac could be its sister,
the redbud is among the first to flower
in April, beating the mazy apple by weeks.

At the edge of my yard
it seems to have bloomed
overnight, constellating itself
with blossoms shaped like the pea's.
A bad translation of red—
rose-purple perhaps,
blooming like a new bruise,
a shadow under the eye.

What carelessness leads
to failures of sight?

At twenty,
I would have taken any name
without question.

2.

Some call it Judas tree
for an old world species
the man was said
to have hung himself from
after naming Jesus with a kiss.

Every word we choose
diffuses the light of a thing.

The way *rose* can mean
dark pink to purplish pink,
medium to purplish red,

what does a kiss disclose?

We have only this spectrum,
the body's poor language.
One touch for love.
Betrayal. Need.

3.

And what *if* the bud is red?
Only the bud. If it changes
like anyone does over time?
Why, then, do I still feel deceived?

4.

As a girl I was taught
that meaning was fixed. It was useless
arguing with my father.
The dictionary made promises,
its demands on us.
A word had walls, like a house.

Fearing correction,
I rebelled in silence,
then by speaking in emblems.

Still, I must have trusted
in *love.*

I am as far from the red bud
as dark lavender
and a little closer to forgiving
by the time the tree blurs
to green,

the underside of each leaf
like flannel to touch
and paler than the surface
exposed to the light.

5.

Red bud, purple flower,
gray green leaf. As if it were that easy
to separate one stage from the next,
as if the ocean could be diagrammed,
a syntax of still water,
rising wave, crest. Or the moon
carrying itself with grace
from crescent to term.

6.

Traveling back and back
to the colorless winter
before the bud ornamented the branch,

I leave summer, a buzz
half-remembered,
ghostly as day moths,
a white lie—

only the falling from is clear.

What is metaphor
but the magician's art,
a woman if not blossom or seed?
The trick is still to unlock the box
from inside.

7.

It would be a long time before I knew
another kind of blossoming
beyond the rosettes
frost makes on the pane.

Tree-about-to-flower,
fading beauty, color burst.

Call it what you will.

The redbud at the edge of my garden
is about to be overcome
by honeysuckle,
about to become something else.

IV

After Dark

She is thinking of the delta
shimmering with tidal and freshwater urgings

as his hand opens on the flat
of her breast bone. So much sediment

there, the Mississippi argues its way
through the bayous, pausing for the ibis,

the tall-legged cypress, the heron
that cannot decide, walking backwards,

it seems, while moving ahead.
A million years of water

in which sturgeon, carp and crustacean
sink and rise with the leaves

of the ancient willow,
half-dissolved root, pungent bone.

In this ambiguous world, both fluid
and firm, she drifts between the blurry borders

of the current, and beyond,
through cottonwood nebulas, pollen, and siftings

of alluvial plain, admitting
love can exceed our intentions,

those levees built against flooding.
But mainly she is struck

by its patient, persistent nature.
The constant nibbling of the river

like a fiddler crab
whose tiny legs (tickling like his beard)

weaken a soft bank until, thunder from afar,
it collapses into water.

Gem City Mine

At the base of the mountain
men are emptying the studded dirt
into trucks. Five dollars
buys three buckets' worth, a pan

and a place at the trough
where the water runs chocolate,
then clear, gravel and silver.
Not knowing ruby from garnet,

emerald from peridot,
you pick up a pail,
emptying handfuls onto the screen.
How would you recognize happiness?

Still you sift: amazonite?
amethyst? searching for something explicit
as the star in the sapphire,
the pearly one, its cornflower blue.

And while you are new at this,
your eyes open wide now, look
for a tell-tale glimmer,
the twinkle of aqua,

of sea-glass green,
the fugitive light that tells you,
yes, I've found something, this
is worth keeping.

Cicada

What is heaven if not this?
The cicada in all its awkwardness,
still the shape of the coffin

it shed on a tree,
rising now
on the pubic threads of its wings.

Hear the escapees—
a sizzling in the limbs and the leaves,
like something's burning

in this summer's heat, erotic,
so unmelodic it hurts to listen.
This is not as I imagined

the born again.
Blunt face. Walleyed,
grotesque even,

as a gargoyle is human,
those the dark has made
find one another.

✑ Midnight

Oh, do not let it unravel—
   this seems less a dream
than before, years ago,
   when you first watched
the eclipse of the moon—

   in a dark cupboard,
one plate stacked against another.

   Now
the earth's slow progress
   is taking forever—

close your eyes
   and feel beneath the lids
the weight of sight,
   nothing's erased—

even when the bodies
   are aligned, the moon
is discernible under the other

   the way something
of the original tongue
   shines through a translation.

Memory, shadow play,

   heart, expanding to enclose
everything felt.

   Including *this*.
The moon coming back,
   your breath returning,
love replenishing itself.

🖋 Another World

*It started raining hard, and we got a little bit
worried. Then it started hailing, and we looked at
each other with a little bit more worry. Then a
window blew out, and someone yelled, "Hit the floor!"
Windows were breaking, bricks were falling and finally it
was almost like we woke up in another world. We
were in the sanctuary, but we could see the sky above us.*
  —Pastor of the Goshen United Methodist
            Church, Piedmont, Alabama

Lying in the dark last night
I wished for a Palm Sunday, a Passover sky—

desert blue. But what bloomed recently
today is sealed in ice:

crab apple and sweet gum.
Snow hooding the daffodils.

In Alabama, a church full of penitents
prays for the Resurrection a week away—

and suddenly the roof
blows off,

a car rolls over,
someone's daughter is gone,

the body we cling to.
And I'm spinning

without an axis again.
Like the million

ticks of the heart,
its counterpoint,

snow changing direction,
loss sings against gain.

47

✍ Women

Women are mostly metamorphic,
  gneiss, marble, schist, slate,
recrystalized only under great heat
  or pressure.
    Or, compare us

to a levee
  keeping the river from the fields.
In flood time, I've heard,
  the wall takes a deep breath
    before going under.

Once, on a train,
  I met a singer who told me
that forced to her third story window by fire
  she was carried faster
    than any scale she had sung

to the sidewalk she hit
  headfirst,
shattering her instrument.
  After the accident of birth,
    people speak of what befalls us

as if from the compound
  of *being* and *falling*
we are made.
  Queen Anne's Lace.
    Black-eyed Susan,

all the wildflowers along the roads
  I love have women's names.
Mid-summer,
  the cicadas singing their praises,
    I am far

48

from those stations we passed,
   New London, Old Saybrook,
outside our window, snow
      filling a sky
         the tincture of smoke.

Trying her new voice,
      she got this close—saying, *look,*
you can hardly see the scars.
      White water. Fire. Whatever vise
         bears down upon us.

Long afterwards,
   I see her jump,
dark head, arms, legs:
      an eighth, sixteenth note
         quickening as she falls.

When the Light Changes

A clear idea of the thing
dims, love,

the way the line
I am writing ends in hesitation,

a body floats
before going down, forever

perhaps, or moving on—
one clear stroke, and the swimmer

is propelled again over the waves.
It's the question that keeps returning

even as the man, shaking the water
from his luminous torso,

emerges, and in a few confident strides
moves across the sand,

then lies down, face up,
and closes his eyes to the glare.

Through the lid, the sun is annular.
And what was animate—

umbrellas tilting, a yellow chair folding in
upon itself, the children at play—

is imageless to the man
hounded by a cry, the briny odor

of fish rot, an oiled thigh.
Jealousy blindfolds like this.

What I ask myself now
is how I could have been so oblivious

the morning of the eclipse.
I had heard the predictions,

but even when my desk darkened
and I had to turn a light on at noon to read,

I was as baffled as I would be later
when you came to me

with your accusations,
your confidence in portents,

the shadow of someone
coming between us.

✒ Blondin

Last night when you touched me
I thought of the great French tightrope walker,
Blondin, crossing the Niagara River on a cord
no thicker than a wrist. We'd had dinner,
a little wine, as he had the evening he dreamed
he stood above the falls. Dazzled,
night clothes dropping from his body,
he felt pinions spread from his ankles
and arms. In the beginning, he couldn't see
what lay beneath him, though he knew
it was more than air or water, the riddling dark
along with a chorus of well-wishers
and disbelievers making him dizzy.
Finally he saw someone small as a child
coming from the other shore.
Closer, he recognized himself,
a man in a blue tunic
with a balancing pole in his hands.
Forget everything else, he said,
and, like that, he began doing scales
on the span of manila hemp.
Now he was blindfolded,
then walking on stilts.
Nothing could distract him
as he felt his way through that space.
Not the guy wires, which were invisible,
the wind between countries.
Not even the fireworks going off all around him,
the blaze of ooh's and ah's from the crowd.

Snake Road

Mud, green vine, and ringneck.
A cottonmouth still the mottled
colors of youth.

Even the blue and black racers
linger on the sunny gravel,
out of harm's way for a while,

the month the road's closed
to boys who count the crushed
in one swift ride through.

What do snakes dream
as they doze halfway between
duckweed-covered swamp and the bluff?

Sugar trapped in the leaves,
sienna, sunset and harvest:
equinox is upon us,

what is unfinished can wait—
bonemeal for the iris, those bulbs
left unplanted for months.

Such limited ambition,
the path through hickory and oak
to a crevice above winter's drifts.

I had thought migration
the heroism of delicate creatures
crossing great distances:

hummingbirds and monarchs
airborne to Mexico. The Arctic tern
ranging from pole to pole.

And so, of simple survival,
I made my myths.
When the snakes wake from their naps

I will follow them
up the bluff
where they'll sleep a long sleep,

done for a season with change.
Coiled, in orbits beyond
blizzards and wind,

they'll forget their way there,
the swamp where they started,
forest on either side.

And what would it hurt
to slow the heart down
like a wintering thing?

To say,
this far I have come.
I will rest for a while.

༻ Faultline

It wasn't at all what she had imagined.
This gentle rocking. As if she'd been awakened

at sea, the boat she found herself in
at ease in the waves, a swallow

dipping on currents of air,
darker than the still dark morning.

Elsewhere, the earth is riven.
At the epicenter, the wounded spill

from their beds, the desert's cleaved
along a fault, every beautiful surface

masking its death.
But more than that,

it's the slipperiness of things,
what you thought you could trust

coming up like a coin
on the other side,

the way some words are reversible.
Like *cleave*. Or *close*. *Close?* Out of context

how would you know how to say it?
And even here, before dawn,

lying next to her lover
several hundred miles from the quake

she's not sure
which part of speech applies.

His eyes, sometimes green,
sometimes blue;

her mind with him, then in another season
watching the leaves turn to wine.

Where is it written
that intimacy must end?

Outside, oleander comes alive
in the courtyard, desert willow, tamarisk,

while within, where they lie,
the snowy motes lift in the first light,

lift, and fall, fall where they will,
shimmering.

A NOTE ON THE AUTHOR

Allison Funk, born in 1951, received a B.A. from Ohio Wesleyan University and an M.F.A. in Writing from Columbia University. She has been the recipient of a fellowship from the National Endowment for the Arts and the George Kent Prize from *Poetry*. Her poems have appeared in *The Best American Poetry, 1994, Poetry, Poetry Northwest,* and other journals. Her first book of poems, *Forms of Conversion,* was published in 1986. She teaches at Southern Illinois University at Edwardsville.

A NOTE ON THE PRIZE

The Samuel French Morse Poetry Prize was established in 1983 by the Northeastern University Department of English in order to honor Professor Morse's distinguished career as teacher, scholar, and poet. The members of the prize committee are Francis C. Blessington, Joseph deRoche, Victor Howes, Ruth Lepson, Stuart Peterfreund, P. Carey Reid, and Guy Rotella.